ALTAMIRA

Also by Myra Sklarew

Poetry

5 New Poets, John Holmes, editor (Poets' Workshop Associates, Medford, Mass. 1954)

In the Basket of the Blind (Chapbook, Cherry Valley Editions, 1975)

From the Backyard of the Diaspora (Dryad Press, 1976, 1981)

Blessed Art Thou, No-One (Chowder Chapbooks, 1982)

The Science of Goodbyes (University of Georgia Press, 1982, 1983)

The Travels of the Itinerant Freda Aharon (Chapbook, Water Mark Press, 1985)

Altamira (Washington Writers Publishing House, 1987, 2022)

Eating the White Earth (Tag Press, 1994, Hebrew tr.)

Lithuania: New & Selected Poems (Azul Editions, 1995, 1997)

The Witness Trees (Cornwall Books, 2000, 2008)

Harmless (Mayapple Press, 2010)

If You Want to Live Forever (Chapbook, Winterhawk Press, 2012)

The Courage to Fight Violence Against Women, (Karnac Press, 2017)

Akedah: The Binding of Isaac (Politics & Prose Opus Publishing 2021)

Essays

Over the Rooftops of Time (State University of New York Press, 2003)

Fiction

Like a Field Riddled by Ants (Lost Roads Publishers, 1988)

Nonfiction

The Journey of Child Development: Selected Papers of Joseph Noshpitz, M.D. Co-editor with Bruce Sklarew (Routledge: Taylor & Francis, 2010)

The Junk Dealer's Daughter by Sarah Blacher Cohen, Co-editor with Merrill Leffler (Dryad Press, 2012)

The Power of Witnessing (Routledge: Taylor and Francis, 2012),
　　Chapter: "Leiser's Song"
Invitation to a Country Called Aging: Co-author with Patricia
　　Garfinkel (Politics & Prose, 2018)
Healing Trauma: The Power of Listening, edited by Evelyn Jaffe
　　Schreiber (IPBooks, 2018), Chapter: "Trauma Made Manifest:
　　Its Persistent Forms"
A Survivor Named Trauma: Holocaust Memory in Lithuania
　　(SUNY Press, 2020)

In Manuscript
Lie Perfectly Still: Essays on Mortality and Healing
Sing, Little Collar Button: Poetry Separation (a prose piece in 10
　　parts)
Remember (a play cast as music)
The Refusal (novel set in Greek village)
The Girl Who Could Not Stop Talking (a children's book)

Previous Praise

From the Backyard of the Diaspora

Myra Sklarew's first book of poems...speaks with quiet truth, unusual in these times, of a vision of wholeness; and it speaks, too, with the wholeness of vision. The book is about the dispersion of the Jews...about the inability to communicate with others, and about exile even from oneself...about the process of healing—the movement home, towards Jerusalem, towards integration in society, towards completion of self.

　　　　—Nancy Prothro, *Sybil-Child*

Superimposed on biblical myth and 20th century atrocities in Europe is the figure of the Human dispersed within herself, obtaining relief and strength not from the remnants of a religion, but from the imagination. The two perspectives intertwine repeatedly; the imagination borrows from tradition...and the tradition maintains its stubborn foothold weathering (if not revitalized in) a distortion of itself.... The poems are a substitute for spiritual language that has lost its vitality.

　　　　—Ron Slate, *Chowder Review*

The Science of Goodbyes

Leavings and losses, those constant ingredients in our lives, are unfolded by the poet in their variety and added to the store of valid human experience. Objects surrounding us every day, insights guided by Jewish ritual and history, relationships remembered or hoped for are evoked...This is Sklarew's first full-length collection since 1975 and one of the most appealing, strikingly intelligent books this reviewer has seen in months.

　　　　—Inge Judd, *Library Journal*

Over the Rooftops of Time: Jewish Stories, Essays, and Poems

The author's personality, as it emerges in these various writings, is extremely appealing and sympathetic. She is searching, does not shrink from self-revelation, is sensitive to the pain of the world, and, overall, is supremely perceptive and intelligent in what she has to say.

–Judith R. Baskin, editor of *Women of the Word: Jewish Women and Jewish Writing*

Like a Field Riddled by Ants

I have been following Myra's Sklarew's poetry for many years, and I am aware of its continual deepening into forms of daring and manifest freedom... I recognize how she is quietly extraordinary.

–Cynthia Ozick

ALTAMIRA

POEMS

Myra Sklarew

Washington Writers' Publishing House
Washington, D.C.

COVER DESIGN by Andrew Sargus Klein
TYPOGRAPHY by Barbara Shaw

Library of Congress Control Number: 2022938469
ISBN: 978-1-941551-30-1

WASHINGTON WRITERS' PUBLISHING HOUSE
2814 5th Street, NE, #1301
Washington, D.C. 20017

For Olympia Lucette Renaud and Elle Josephine Renaud
My twin messengers of light

Contents

Foreword by Jona Colson

JUST LIKE THE CAVES OF ALTAMIRA in Northern Spain, timeless and inspiring, this collection of poetry is one to be celebrated, studied, and admired. In the title poem, Myra Sklarew asks, "And if I should give / you these words / and you are not there to receive them / so they become part / of what is unused / and moves on?" Lucky for us, we are here to receive and celebrate this new edition of *Altamira*, which has been out-of-print for nearly three decades. In 1987, the Washington Writers' Publishing House first published *Altamira* by Myra Sklarew, her third full-length collection. The press, now in its 48th year, honors writers from the D.C., Maryland, and Virginia area, and Myra Sklarew is one of the most revered and well-known poets and poetry teachers—locally and internationally.

I met Myra Sklarew when I enrolled in the Master of Fine Arts program at American University—a program she helped found in 1980 and is still the only MFA in Creative Writing Program in Washington, D.C. When I started taking classes in 2001, she had been the co-director for many years and had an intimidating reputation as a tough teacher. However, she was also generous and tender with her students, offering feedback and encouragement as I discovered in many poetry and literature workshops with her. When I began reading her work, I started with *Altamira*, and I was taken with its intimacy, craft, and emotion—and the poems remain timeless and immediate, like Altamira's caves.

In "Hieroglyphic," she writes, "Once a girl / innocently typing / put the wrong word / on the page/ and in a flash / changed my career." Many of the poems in this collection are a glyph seeking its interpreter as the reader wanders through landscapes known and unknown. These fervent, and often, aching poems of be/longing, live on the margins, and inquire about departures, arrivals, and returns. In the poem, "Looking at Men," Sklarew writes, "Yesterday, a man asked me / why I was traveling alone. / If he were my husband, / he would not permit me to / go away." This poem highlights one of the many questions Sklarew asks—what are the limits of gender or its expectations? Why does someone have the privilege and others do not? What is it to be an outsider in another culture or religion?

Poems in this collection investigate belonging and place as Sklarew invites us into other countries, languages, and families, as in the poem, "At the Syrian Border," where she writes, "Walking between two mine fields / I pretend I am a tourist here." She voices love for the "old country" and questions the "new." What is home? What is language? Is home where we are born, or where we are buried? A place where we have lived and given our strength and best years? Some are born speaking one language, and then die speaking another. Many times, we do not decide where home is, and Sklarew investigates the emotional and physical borders that often decide for us.

Having trained in science, Sklarew's curiosity of science and poetry explode and question semantics and nature. She studied biology at Tufts, specifically bacterial viruses at Cold Spring Harbor Biological Laboratory, and later at Yale Medical School, she did research on memory and the prefrontal cortex. Hence, she taught a course that I took at American University on Literature and Memory, and I was struck by her instruction of how memory is formed, informed, and changed in creative work. In *Altamira*, the poem, "Walking," highlights her imaginative and scientific brilliance: the narrator finds "a white egg/ too large for a bird." Then, mistakenly is answered that the egg is from a "wild dog," and she imagines "the wild dog / hatching from the white egg. / I see him flying." Sklarew inverts the expectation of the word—dog. How do we know what a dog is? How do we define what things are? The play of imagination and definition are deft—one of Sklarew's many incredible gifts to us.

For you, dear reader, if you know Myra Sklarew and her work, or you do not, I invite you to let her take you on a journey to other places—physical and emotional. I ask that you receive these words of a masterful poet, teacher, and human. May these poems connect us all.

Jona Colson
Washington, DC
2022

Grateful acknowledgement is made to the following publications:

Science/82: "Forms, lowly organized, long enduring"
Science/83: "Hieroglyphic"
Reconstructionist: "Map," "At the Syrian Border," "Crossing Over"
Women Poets: The South: "There"
The New York Times: "Refusal"
Crosscurrents: "At Yehuda's Wedding"
Shirim: "Transplant," For the Sake of a Poem"
Seneca Review: "After Stalin"
Songs from Unsung Words: Science/85: "Beetles, wingless in Madeira," "Cabbage, varieties of, crosses," "Forms, lowly organized, long enduring"
The Denver Quarterly: "Dreaming of Rain"
Sheep Meadow Press: A Celebration of Stanley Kunitz: "At the Syrian Border" 1986

A grant from the National Endowment for the Arts in 1981 provided time for work on this manuscript. A stay at Yaddo during the summer of 1984 provided time and space to come back to my own work and contact with composers, artists and writers.

Ann Darr, given an unwieldy collection of poems, found the true shape of this book, its arrangement and underlying architecture. As she did with The Science of Goodbyes. She has my profound gratitude.

For Jean Nordhaus, my lost sister of childhood whom I found again through poetry—in celebration of *A Bracelet of Lies*.

The Washington Writers' Publishing House gratefully acknowledges the support of Laura Brylawski which contributed to making the publication of this series of books possible.

For the Sake of a Poem: for Moshe Dor

A man asks
for the sake of a poem
starting somewhere in him
the name of the bird
just now landing

on water,
its speckled points
like vowel marks
of his own language.

The woman observes
it is neither duck
nor goose.
Tarnagolet H'Gam,
she tells him.
Chicken-of-the-Pond.

And he takes that name
because she has given it,
puts the bird
with its colors
of the wilderness
he is exiled from
into his poem.

The man has that bird caught
inside the cage
of his poem,
the poem caught
inside many books,
here and in other countries.

Poets whisper its name.
But the name
rests uneasily
on the waters
of their speech.

One day the man opens
a book about birds
and sees the Tarnagolet H'Gam
his faithful wife
has given him.

And he knows
in that instant of recognition
the name she has given him
is wrong.

The woman tries
to tell him
how all he needed
was her answer
so his poem
could go on
forming itself,

so the bird falling
falling from her tongue,
the laborious name
swollen and huge
could hold in air

for as long
as it needed
until water could take it,
until the poem
carefully weighted
had all it could bear
and still float.

The Door to That Room

Looking at Men

Yesterday, a man asked me
why I was traveling alone.
If he were my husband,
he would not permit me to
go away. It says in the
Koran the woman is the
comfort of the man's
body. * The men took
turns picking leeches off
each other's bodies. When
the war ended, the smell
of fresh soap made them
vomit. * A man and his
son and a horse. The father
says: Get up on the horse.
As they journey they pass
a jeering crowd. How can
you let your old father walk
while you ride? they ask
the boy. The father climbs
up behind his son and they
continue on their journey.
They pass a group of people
working in a field. How can
you both ride, wearing out
your old horse? they ask.
In the end the father and
son carry the horse. *
I watch a man quicken as he
crosses a mine field, as he
climbs into a bunker and
takes up his submachine
gun. * Replacements

7

have come for instruction.
The sergeant picks up a
smooth metal ring. Do you
know, he looks into their
boys' faces, what these
can do? * Beneath me
a man's head is the only
marker as he walks the
labyrinth of trenches; this
one's never seen war. He
feels the earth around his
body, the closest he's come
to his own grave. * At
night a man smokes a
cigarette when he cannot
sleep. These are true
stories of a personal nature.
*   From letters I know
how a man wishes to be seen.
From sleeping with him I know
how a man is. * Under
me a man holds perfectly
still to see how long he can
stay inside me without
coming. * A man, partly
blind, touches my back lightly
with one finger to learn
where he is in this world.
I mistake it for love. *
Lady, a man calls to me,
beautiful lady, if only you
knew what you wanted, I would
show it to you.

At Yehuda's Wedding

At Yehuda's wedding
the children
hold the canopy up

In our lives
the children come
to hold us up

over their heads
like cloth and glass

They wear us
like a tallit
We are knotted
and fringed

We have come
from the four comers
of the earth

And under their feet
our hearts
like the wine glass
the bridegroom
crushes with his strong
heel

What Hasanin M' Barak Said

If you ask
how many are buried here,
I must ask you how many liters
of water are in the sea.

At their doorposts they kept
nailed a passage
in strange script which
they touched
with their fingers
and brought to their lips
whenever they entered.

They taught us
to say this blessing
over bread and this
over wine and this for the slaughter
of animals.
And why did you not recite
the blessing yourself
over the tea just then?

When they left us
we embraced them like brothers
for they had given us pleasure
as we had them.

We have taken their names
for our children.
When we call our sons,
our daughters, we carry
in our voices
a small song of their names.

We do not know
what became of them.
Have you seen them
on your way in
to this place?

Ouarzazate, Morocco 1981

After Stalin

I thought
there was nothing
left of them

That when
they were finished off
with sabers and starvation
it was the end
Once and for all

But I was wrong—
Me with my doomsday mother
riding on my back
pointing out the half-empty world

They have pieced them
together out of old sleeves
a nail and a hank of hair
Put the discarded eyeglasses
back on their faces
and reconstructed
the world

Never mind the little mother
with her legs wrapped around my ribs
with her shoes battering
against me trying to lead the way

When the nations
swelled up
and spilled over
these used
and pieced together ones
these sons and daughters
of the dead

rose up and came forth
carrying the loose pages
that were their mothers
the broken-down sentences
still talking
who are called their fathers

At the Syrian Border

Walking between two mine fields
I pretend I am a tourist here: What trees,
I say. What mountains. I mouth
slogans bitter as a salt sea.

The wind feeds on the basalt rock.
Under every eucalyptus there is
the yawning shadow of a bunker. My people
is an armed camp.

I remember a boy who made a bridge
of his body for the others to climb across.
They turned him into air and fire and earth.
And here is the place where a father

let his child down a knotted sheet
like Jacob, only not going up.
One child by one child down the ladder
of knots and when he himself climbed

down for the last time he found each one
murdered. 0 Jacob let us put away
our strange gods. My people is an armed
camp. Her sons wear old faces.

Dreaming of Rain

1

Nothing is left
but the tracks of the water
and the roar
the rain made as it withdrew
from sleep's house
like a tidal wave that turns
on its heel and departs
in a single motion
leaving the floor of the sea
suddenly naked.

2

It was a good, a drenching
rain. I knelt on the earth
just before it began and took up
a sample in my hands: quartz
and mica shone on my fingers
and the dry dust fell
back among the seed coats.
How is it the wild
strawberry finds sustenance
here? The notched petals
of the dogwood are drawn tight
as though someone pulled
on a thread.

3

You touch the dust
under your shoes and ask: Am I
made of this?
And the water
answers.

4

Many nights the rain visited
like that, opening itself
to the earth, its sac of waters
prelude to the rebirth.
And we stood
helplessly by in our doorways
sending our fingers
like Pharaoh's daughter out
into the river
to claim what the water
had washed down to us.

5

I see by a cloud that has slipped
into the earth
the rain has been here during the night.
But we had no sign of it while we slept,
only the seed coats falling
silently to the roof.

6

When the water came, pitched
like stones, we did not stop
dreaming of it;
we fell asleep eagerly
taking the dust of the dry earth
with us into the deepest room.

The Door to That Room

Say you were born in a chicken
   coop. The first thing you
   remember is looking out from
   your slot. The bantam cocks
   are crowing in the next bin.

Say you were comforted by scaly
   yellow legs rising in a ring
   around you. That you flew
   off the perch with your
   feathers whirring like there
   were motors inside.

For a time you got separated
   from the others. High up
   in a room off a hall
   you spelled out your name
   on the ceiling and the morning
   sun came to fill in
   the letters with light.

Each road ends at the door
   to that room. Just as the light
   begins to withdraw from
   the ceiling and long before
   the first star comes centering
   itself in the dark window,
   hovering uncontrollably like
   the body's shudder.

Below, doors open. A man and a
  woman make promises they will
  abandon in the first light.
  A dog barks out in his dream.
  The red fox makes his rounds
  past the woodpile.

In the schoolyard, a girl standing
  on her head watches a red stain
  spread across the bottom of her
  gymsuit. A boy throws a rock
  into a yellow jacket's nest and
  sets you down onto it. You run,
  bees coming off your head like
  a jet stream rushing east.

You knit a khaki scarf twenty feet
  long for your uncle in North
  Africa. This is during the war.
  He comes back alive, still stuttering,
  with perfume in narrow vials.

You have a radio so large you could
  walk into it. On a wall high up
  in a world you haven't come to,
  a boy takes off his clothes
  and lies down.

Soldiers with machine guns patrol
   just beneath him. He isn't starving
   yet, his father hasn't been gassed.
   He trades his ration of bread
   for a book.

For months you dream of shark, barracuda,
   dolphin. Your father comes home one
   night with a wooden barrel. He digs
   a hole among his tomato plants and
   sets the barrel into the earth.

He fills it with water and goldfish.
   The water leaks out between the
   staves. The fish glue themselves
   against the bottom of the barrel.

In that country, a mother and father
   sit halfway up the stairs getting
   the news. The ashes of their dead
   sisters and brothers float up the
   staircase and fall onto their bodies.

The Polish piano teacher calls out
   to the Mother of God every time
   you put your fingers on the keyboard.
   You hide on the floor of her closet
   holding her green satin shoes. On
   the way home your sister will try
   to lose you again.

Somewhere in the house a woman is
  crying. The mirrors are covered
  with black cloths. The lid of the
  piano is closed.

You do not kiss the face of the
  grandmother in the box that has
  two holes in the bottom so she
  can leak out.

Nothing will be the same again.
  The father with the barrel and
  the fish has gone into the earth.
  On Main Street, Fortunato is still
  standing in his doorway waiting
  for the next fire.

And Vinnie Gallo is sliding all
  the way down to the bottom of
  the scale on his alto sax.

Crossing Over

Childhood

My childhood
was not generous;
its strict hours
laid out
in a grid
across the week.

Whoever thinks
his childhood
is friendly?
That we are
greeted with cakes
and open arms?

Once on a table
in a hospital ward
the lilacs
gave off a mysterious
air, their odor
all I had of home.

My mother stood
in the street below
without seeing me
as I waved
from my glass cubicle
like a war criminal.

First Language

I go over it. It does not yield.
The same stiff afternoon: the music
rising to my mother's room.
                    I have forsaken
the score-notes advancing
like some rigid herd, their round faces
mounting parallel tracks.

In an attic space bought from the skull's
own room, another tune has started up,
seized my arms, commanded me. My fingers
know this song too, yet find their way
in it as it goes, unknowing.
And in this passage, I gladly abandon myself
and have lifelong.

She calls out. I close off that music
and go up the stairs. My first language
this, before words. I cannot say
the song I've made. All afternoon
in that high room she begged to know. I stood
before her clenched shut, a black bead
wedged on the staff
like some animal head caught.

I dared not look at the rocking chair—
The blind ones imbedded there
who twisted on their root
and came apart.
She could not let me go nor would I
release myself.
            On the piano the pages
of the true song stayed open. The chair
is in my room now, tame as any tame thing
can be until the blind past comes lurching forth.
To this day I have not told the nature
of the song I made.

A Place

We have come to a place
where language ends, the words
short-circuit on the page.
Which word can contain a boy
broken into or a girl laid down
on the packed earth of a schoolyard
in September, her body taking
the fists of a boy screaming Jew Jew.
This is not a poem of sorrow
or complaint.
Not a poem to find out
why a child
in a lonely basement
offered her breasts to us.

Transplant

They used to bring
a bit of soil
from the old country
to the new

Or at burial
a handful
of sand
from the desert
to accompany
the dead
on the long journey
from diaspora
to resurrection

Or now
without soil
or sand
seed
from the inner courtyard
dispersed
between the legs
of the exiled

Becoming a Jew

When I was born
they called me a Jew.
I hurried to put on
the shoes
of a Jew. I hurried
to put on the hat
of a Jew. But still
I wasn't a Jew.
In the mirror I tried
to read the difference
between us. But my red
hair, my pale skin
refused to explain it.
They asked if I
believed in their God.
I put a star
on a chain at my neck
but like the dress
of my sister
it did not fit.
They gave my sister
a cloth badge
and she sewed it on
with perfect stitches,
with fine black thread.
They took my sister
away to the center
of our city and left
her there without food
or water. For seven days.

We did not see
my sister again.
The young boys began
sailing their bodies
through the glass
windows like kites.
My father's tears
on the stone step.
My father's name.

Crossing Over

When my first child tore
loose from me
the old woman cautioned: Bite off
her nails with your teeth
and bury them in the earth.

In the fall of that year
the feet of Abraham
went overhead—Isaac his son
at his side, the wood
for the burnt offering sprouting
leaves at one end, root hairs
at the other.
And the fire
in the father's hands
sent up its bright alphabet,
a signal to Sarah.
In the narrow passage between intent
and act,
the angel's call
and the confusion of the ram.

Here, on our side
in the Feast of Booths
the trees
have put out too much fruit
as though after the long drought
they might not survive: black walnuts,
acorns not yet ripe, tough capsules
propelled through the air
without letup;
the knobs leave their imprint
on the soles of our feet.

In the firmament
between worlds the guardian
of invalid prayers—those uttered
with the lips, the heart
dragging behind—urges us
to delay awhile.

What doors must close
before this one can open?
And which angel
rises up through the brickwork
of sapphire
to bid farewell
to this child torn out
of the distance
like the leaf of the ash I tear off
to find
in back of each green shape
a seed
trawling in the morning light.

Map

I made a map from the parts
of your life and I carry it around
like an idiot child.

It clings to my side, pointing
dumbly at the world. Poor scholar,
it has forgotten so much:

who goes before Abraham and which
brother killed which, who dressed
in the skin of a goat.

I tell my map to make a line
through all points above sea level;
I tell it blue for oceans, green

for lowlands. But it only shows
which territories were lost
and which sons.

My map doesn't know how many years
between this night and the one
where we said goodbye.

There are so many things I wanted
to ask you, so many things
I have tried to tell you.

Altamira

1

For this is my own.
    And if you ask
for my unveiling of it,
if together we must take
it into the light,
surely it will disguise
itself.
    Once we gave over
our bodies to others
saying: Here, you may
have this, we will not
notice. Though somewhere
it pained us and we knew.

2

    Words. Keeping them
out of the light
of the others. Like the cave
at Altamira
which the sunlight
and breathing have ruined,
coating the bison
with the newer air, causing
the lines to grow
indistinct.
    It was, after all ,
distinctness we sought
in those days, some way
to pull apart without tearing,
some way to live.

3

    Words, we dwelt
in them. A small enough
armor against the others.
And the words clung
to us as though
they had come from afar
to rescue us.
    They had something
to tell, some portion
of themselves to impart.
How could we say to another
what the words wished us
to know. There are many
forms of betrayal.

4

    After you entered into
my life and became part
of me, I rode out
in the darkness and went
away slowly so as not
to disturb the configuration
we made,
    as though I had left
only lately the bed
of a lover, my body still
bearing his mark, his
seed clinging to me
having sought me out
and found me
and my body holds it
as long as it can live.

5

Oh bought and paid for
Muse, how quickly the
punishing words come
to erase
whatever is being
made, whether in sunlight
or cave.
      This commerce, simple
purchase of what is left
before time leaves
us, what harm could
come of it.
      Yet the voice rises
in the archaic scale
making its judgements—court
and jury.

6

And if I should give
you these words
and you were not there
to receive them
so they would become part
of what is unused
and moves on,
like the bison hurtling
across the roof
of a great lateral chamber
toward their own past,
what harm would be done?

7

Or if something just
now should cause you to turn
away. Too late for the words
to turn back, to become
a lament or a silence.
Or if you should call
for them. To say that you
gladly awaited them. That
terrifying possibility. If
they were to shed their names,
their substance going out
into the new air. If you were
to take only their constant
arrivals. That.

Refusal

In August
you died
And in September
the year
turned around
regardless
In October
the leaves
on signal
depart
their trees
On signal
the flies
grow sluggish
in the window
well
Frost crystals
line up
on the glass
Only I
am recalcitrant
refusing
to put away
the leather band
that circled
your wrist
the clockhouse
with its contents
fallen
out of time

There

Under the dead surface you
surge toward me and then draw
back. What realm supports you now

and what necessity leaves me
struggling after you here
on the surface, parted
by this membranous divide.

I enfold you, what of you chooses
to come this close.
By this method you enter my body
and are lost in me.

For is it not so that I fall
asleep with my hands on my own body.
Or that my words going out can find
no suitable place for landing.

And when I stand in the company
of others, when I have gathered
my clothing about me and risen

to say good night I am surprised
by the weight of the cold
which I draw about my own shoulders.

Or when you withdrew from me
in a day not so different
from this one, your skull seemed

to shrink between my two hands. This
is the world. This is the world
with its circuitry ranging between there
and here like an animal grazing.

In the season of your death I cannot
enter the room for the saying of a thing
without encountering the danger
of fusion. Past and future support me

on either side like two crutches
while in the doorway the shadow
of my life goes on ahead
testing the unknown ground.

February 18, 1974

The Falling Out

The Falling Out

Penelope to Laertes

1

Though we had a falling out
it was your shroud
I told them I was weaving: even
the suitors would not
have wanted me to bury you
without it.

I always wondered: was it you
encouraged your son
to go off after a woman
he said he loved.

Old man, you had an eye
for women yourself: four wives
and a share you helped yourself to,
spoils of a city you sacked.
And did you love women?
Or was it something else
drew you to them so assiduously?

"They keep a nestegg,"
you told me once, testing me
to find out where I stood,
"so when things go sour
they'll have a way to hold
their heads up."

2

And when your son left
on that foolish mission
you took his part
though I was the one
abandoned.

I went on
with my handiwork, pulling
one thread
through another, your name
on the death I was weaving.

One by one his companions
bequeathed him their returns
and in his one embrace
crowded all of theirs.

They say he nurtured
a longing to return
despite the way Calypso
worked on him to erase
all sign of Ithaca.

Was it the idea held him
sway more than his memory
of a wife, any shape I made
in his mind's eye.

Whereas I could not change
sufficiently for him
in those days, Laertes,
oh how I am water now
and leopard, serpent, even a high
and leafy tree. Outwitting
suitors is good training.

3

Oh unsaved Laertes, squandered
on death, I'll take no drug
to regulate the shape
of this fear, for if I am made
to forget sorrow,

so all the adventures
of your life will wander from me
and walk into the sea and go
silently under.
Only Helen quieted pain
and strife this way.

Do you remember the day
you took my place at the loom,
your long legs pumping
the wooden struts that raised
and lowered the warp?
Our laughter rose above the din
the suitors made and afterwards,
Laertes, more son than father,
you took my arm and led me
in a simple dance.

4

It came to nothing,
his setting out,
all those returns.
Odysseus left a son
in that great distance.
Circe's child.

And that boy laid claim to him.
Oedipus was innocent
compared to this one: a shade
twisting and turning in the eye
of his own rage. Half boy,
half god, wily and dangerous
as a tide.

He took, unwittingly,
his father.
The gods knew.
And Telemachus,
his true heart perjured
by this news.

But you escaped, old man.
You did not have to witness
the murder. Though you would say
something about adventure,
the way your son broke
from you, a limb
from its trunk, and went
his way.

5

When I saw all that bluster
turned into the earth,
your shroud and casket floating
like the rectangular dark pupil
of a goat's eye against

the golden iris,
I found it difficult
to believe
you could have anything to do
with such a grave.

Where are you, Laertes?
The gravediggers keep gazing up
at the sun: they want to get
this over with. But custom
is custom; we aren't done yet
with our rituals,

If you were here
you'd be on the side of these men,
I know, learning
their names.

They keep lifting the earth
onto their shovels. They try
to lower you into the ground.
But we detain them;
the gods alone know why.
What's done is done.

6

When we came home
from burying you,
a green parrot turned up
in the laurel tree.

Was it you,
restless, not settled
into the earth. It was
your first night
in the ground, after all.

Come here, Odysseus called.
Tell me
what you see, your son
urged me.

And sure enough
in the twisted branches
of the laurel, a green bird
far too heavy for those narrow
limbs sat there.

7

Where you are
evening is closing down
in a hammer lock.
Here, a sun puling
in its cradle of light refuses
to go down. It is
the longest day of the year.

Let the stone which weighed down
the heddle of my loom
be the same stone
I bring to your grave.

The stone
of bitter gall
I wore in those years.
Oh I nurtured it.

My anger split apart
took up residence in you;
else how could I go on
loving your son.

I put off my anger now.
The shroud is hard, finished
against my will,
the years woven into it
like stones.

June-October, 1985

Walking

Three o'clock:
the hawkweed is pointing
toward the sun.

I put my foot down
softly on the earth
not to disturb it.

Above me a plane
dips its wing
into blue.

Along the path
I find a white egg
too large for a bird.

What is this? I ask Maria,
holding out the huge
broken cup.

From wild dog, she tells me
without hesitating.
Wild dog. From the woods.

I imagine it, the wild dog
hatching from the white egg.
I see him flying, his tail

wagging cheerfully.
I say to her: wild dog.
She brings me down.

Duck. Not dog. She looks
at me strangely. That I would
believe such a thing.

Return

The taste of dust
is on my tongue. July
has set foot
in Mekounida again.
And during the night
the wind came up
carrying away
the skenipas swollen
with samples
of my blood they will
exchange later
for that of some unsuspecting
goat on a hillside.
Toula has set down
her embroidery
to gaze at the old woman
in black waiting
at the bus stop, her skirts
raised up to the heavens
in a mad offering—this one,
she will live forever.
And the young beauty
has given birth
to a son with no expression
at all whom she leaves
for her father—it is his
child after all—while she
runs in the fields
with her sisters and
brothers, as though
her real beauty had not
been edged away by
something new, a look
in the eyes which speaks
openly of disaster.

Letter to the Village Elder

Barba Yiorgi, when you write
to me, it sounds
as if you're addressing
your own fate. Ἀγαπημένη μας
Μίρα, you begin. My beloved fate,
you say, using my name.

And though I have asked
for news
of the three goats tethered
beneath the mulberry tree, bundles
of sorghum you've cut
from the lower
field hanging from the branches
for each of them,
you ask about the three
generations of my family instead,
and about my health three times.

And to my questions
about the hens
and the beautiful daughter
of Yiorgos and about
your grandson Stamatis who drives
a tank in a new war,
you will only speak of the three suns
which shine in your yard.

And while you avoid all
my questions, three goats
pick clean
your pockets filled with almonds
for Christina.
And three fates
are at work, one turning
the thread of your life
upon her spindle, one measuring
its length
and a third
with her terrible shears
poised over the spun thread.

News

This morning,
a sack of garbage
in my left hand
and just after I slammed
the door hard with my right,
I stood before
my empty house,
my unapproachable empty
house and could not
get in.

Like my history
which does not open
to take me in,
my unapproachable
history
making its mark on me
while it drives me
across a border
up into the foothills
of another age.

But I am faithful,
making my rounds, telling
what it means
to be a Jew, a woman.
Soon I will tell
the giraffes how it feels
to have the ruminating
soul of a goat, the larynx
of a hyena, to have
the narrow stringy legs
of an ostrich.

Once I was myself,
standing in a field
as I did
this morning,
only a blue sky, the sun.
No airplanes traveling
the perimeter
like runners in an ancient
Roman race. No history,
no news.

Interval

We know
it is only a matter of time
before the distance
collapses in on us,
before we feel
the fur of the world:

                       a train
bearing its cargo
of hands
holding our ankles down
while we strain
with our necks
for air

or an innocent helicopter
calmly patrolling
the river, brother
to the ones that carry
the wounded
back from the north,
the sky filled up
with their insect shapes.

                      The feet
of the hanged ones
swing over our heads like
brass censers
from their chains.
Our frightened god flies
like a bat
through his cave.

At dawn
a horn will sound;
we dance on
numbed by a music
no revolution has prepared
while out on the floor
of the desert hunger
offers its breast.

December 31, 1984

Where We Are Led

When we stood in the schoolyard that day,
we covered Our Lady of the Woods,
we scrolled it up out of sight and attended
only to the bank of trees flowing away from us
along the watery air, our feet
on the asphalt hopscotch squares. We walked
in the schoolyard
as though we had all stepped out
of a Victorian painting: a few pairs, a small group,
the spaces between us suggesting an endless time.
Alongside us a girl recited her catechism
and the old dog built of peculiarly reconstructed
parts lay in the tall grass, his rheumy eyes
reflecting the trees. It was bluegreen that day.
No one brought a camera. Someone said:
Do you see the school house. In the thin rain.
Someone answered: I pretend it is not there.
Only the trees floating away from us

across the watery air.
And we started again, leaving the house that day,
the front door unlocked, as though at any moment
we would return. We walked out toward the street
and bent low under the branches, bark beneath
our feet, the damp cold of December,
until we came to a clearing, a field and the schoolyard.

In a little it would be totally dark.
It was too warm to snow. The nuns came
out of Our Lady of the Woods and knelt down
in the field, holding their rosaries
against their bodies as if they might take wing.
Everywhere we looked there were dark and light nuns, the field
was covered with them. Though their mouths moved
in prayer, we heard only the sounds their broad sleeves made
as they lifted and lowered their arms.

Use

In those years
when the dark wore us
around its throat
we heard a man say: *I have envied*
plants and stones. I
have envied dogs. Now
we bring that man forth
like a bride
at a wedding. We fill
his arms with flowers
and parade him up
and down the aisle.
We take apart
his words as though
they were small stones
from a wall
and with them
we build ourselves
houses far from the border
where he last saw
his mother alive, far
from the place where
the children lay, their shorn
heads in the crooks
of their arms.

Escape

When you looked up
I was gone,
my sadness small enough
it could fit
into the palm of my left
hand, no place
to come back to
at night.
After that
I traveled freely,
my image cancelled
in the others.
I was light then,
like a nation newly conceived
where they are still trying
to make up
its constitution.
In me
they have not yet found
declarations,
statutes, nor covenant.

Water Tower

Years later
the boy pointed up to a water

tower
You see that

he said
I turned my straight arrow

gaze from the road
but I kept my hands

on the wheel
and looked up

It stood
like the body of a spider

its round belly
jutting out

skinny legs jointed
and holding it up

I've been inside that tower
he told me

I did not
stop driving

The water tower
made a shape in my thought

like a wood-burning
needle

I used to climb
the ladder that spirals

around it
the boy told me

At the top I would pry
open the lock

raise the lid and climb in
I would slip down

into the water
and float

on my belly holding
my breath

in the pitch dark
while the others waited

on the crosspieces
of the ladder

They clung there
like outlines of shapes

on the purine rungs
of the helix

sometimes a piece
of a moon above them

sometimes not even that
while below

we made our way
through an anxious sleep

our dreams grown enormous
with their absence

What was it they looked for
in the dark sentinel

over our town
and what did they find

in the solitary
ritual in that closed space

their baptism
in the waters

that would come down to us
in the morning

when we raised the clear glass
to our lips

and drank in
some part of them

a hair
or a cell sloughed off

a way they would seize us
and claim our attention

I think how we went
to and fro

on the ground never
looking up

into the face
of the world above us

like not seeing
the stars or not hearing

the sounds
a boy's arms make

as they cut
into black water

Conversions

Paleontology

A man
when he looks at a patch
of earth
sees the cities
swarming beneath.

And when he looks
at a mountain
he remembers how the sea
pushed up into peaks
leaving remnants
of sand, coral
and shell
he'll find
when he walks there.

When I look at a face
I see the tribe
spinning toward the surface.
I see the lungfish, his primitive
air bladder barely
keeping enough oxygen
to sustain the bubble
which is saving a place
for our brains.

I see a fish
climbing into a tree,
a cell dividing and rising
to the surface
of the skin
like dreams spun
in the darkness of night
rising upward slowly toward
morning.

Origin of Species

1
Cabbage, varieties of, crosses

The exotic cabbage flower
is tricky, with its pistil
surrounded by bodyguards—
those six stamens—and its
self- supplying pollen.
Stick to mongrel cabbages:
they're less high-strung.

2

Beetles, wingless in Madeira

Was it indolence,
this sitting around
leisurely under wind
lulls, hardly moving
for days, that finally
did it, first shortening
the feathery wing,
weakening the muscle
which ran its tiny motor,
then sending it forever
into disuse?

Lazy Beetle, scientists
call it, but Beetle
took his time getting here,
drifting for centuries
on an old log in the sea.
When he arrived he'd made up
his mind: this was his last
stop, here on the comforting
sands under the sun
in Madeira where the music
was much to his liking.

3

Forms, lowly organized, long enduring

You would not ask,
say, the intestinal
worm to change himself,
to grow an enormous
multilobed brain
scrawled with wrinkles,
to remember perfectly
each place he'd lived
and speak of them all
in clear sentences.
Yet he goes on, making
the most of his visitations,
taking what little comes
his way.

His requirements
are small.
No one asks him to keep
an eye on the children
or sign a check.
He stays confined
to his peculiar
station, just out
of harm's way, not too
much competition,
no chance of a favorable
variation.

Conversions

In the aftermath, when the fire of touching
has died down, when what dared to approach
has withdrawn again to become an edge of color,
a shape partially revealed or a longing,
we come back to occupy this place.

And though we have been here before,
what we do not recognize signals us: the past
as it is filtered through a voice,
the doors and windows of escape,
light thrown across an object like water.

Choose the midnight word or the morning.
God and the executions have gone to join
the others. This is neither punishment
nor enclosure. But a place for something
to begin.

Imagine a circle, draw it with a dark pencil.
Afterward you may lift it off the page
and roll it down a street called infinite space.
A hoop of light to crawl through. Pronounce
its name

and it loses none of its power. Or add it
to the pantomime of nine figures who occupy
the same space in a street we have invented.
They touch. The circle has turned red
and loops across the head of a woman.

All is fixed and silent: a baker, the woman
in black, a man who threatens a girl, the luminous
red ball in the foreground. There is a blue rock here
half buried in the earth. The village women
open their blouses

and take their breasts into their hands
and rub them against the rock tenderly.
Afterward they tear strips of cloth
from their skirts and attach these to the bare tree
of the garden like inscriptions.

Here the fish of the waterbanks can
talk to us. Here stems and twigs have
a language. We begin again to construct a world,
hopeful for what breaks against us, the fire
threading its way among live coals.

The inevitable lacunae: The way our bodies
serve as receptacle for two kinds
of light. Or the distance composed of blue stones
by which one traveling toward us would know
the way.

The drift out of here?
A refusal to speak. Evidence we point
at ourselves like a gun. Or a mask
we wear over our faces, the conversion
taking place behind the immobile placard.

Hieroglyphic

Once a girl
innocently typing
put the wrong word
on the page
and in a flash
changed my career
from physiology
to psychology.
I thought: What if
the same girl
types the place
of my birth
after I die—Baltic
for Baltimore
or writes Black
Forest for White
Mountain as my
family name or instead
of Repose puts down
Poseur? I thought:
What if the cause
of death were a
broken heart
instead of a broken-
down heart?
My last street
on earth Wormwood
instead of Marywood?

Who would argue
my case for me?
Surely some good
professor would come
and read down
the tome of my life
from top to bottom
like Hatshepsut's
hieroglyphs, making up
a wonderful story
from wavy lines
and birds and small
unexpected footprints
erased by the sea.

Myra Sklarew, professor emerita American University, founder of the MFA Program, former president of the Yaddo Artist's Community, studied biology at Tufts University, bacterial viruses at Cold Spring Harbor Biological Laboratory, and did research at Yale Medical School in memory and the prefrontal cortex. Former director of Montgomery County Council of Cooperative Nursery Schools (28 schools) and with the Infant Education Project with NIMH and Home Study, Inc. M.A. from Writing Seminars at Johns Hopkins. Twelve poetry collections include *Lithuania: New and Selected Poems.* Prose collections include: *Like a Field Riddled by Ants, Over the Rooftops of Time, An Invitation to a Country called Aging (with Patricia Garfinkel),* and *A Survivor Named Trauma: Holocaust Memory in Lithuania.* A new collection of essays on science and medicine, *Lie Perfectly Still,* is near completion. In 2011, A Splendid Wake—a project to document poets, poetry movements and literary organizations in the Washington, D.C. area from 1900 to the present—sponsored by the Special Collections Research Center at the Gelman Library, GWU, was organized by local poets. At age 14, with the money she earned ($7) playing piano in a dance band, she went to Birdland to hear the music of the great jazz musicians of her day.

Jona Colson's poetry collection, *Said Through Glass*, won the 2018 Jean Feldman Poetry Prize from the Washington Writers' Publishing House. He is also the co-editor of *This Is What America Looks Like: Poetry and Fiction from D.C., Maryland, and Virginia* (2021). His poems have appeared in *Ploughshares, The Southern Review, The Massachusetts Review* and elsewhere. His translations and interviews can be found in **Prairie Schooner, Tupelo Quarterly,** and *The Writer's Chronicle.* He has received fellowships from the Virginia Center for the Creative Arts and the DC Commission on the Arts and Humanities. He earned his MFA from American University, and he is a professor of ESL at Montgomery College in Maryland and lives in Washington, DC. In 2022, he became co-president with Caroline Bock of the Washington Writers' Publishing House.

More from the Washington Writers' Publishing House

2020 Fiction Award-winner

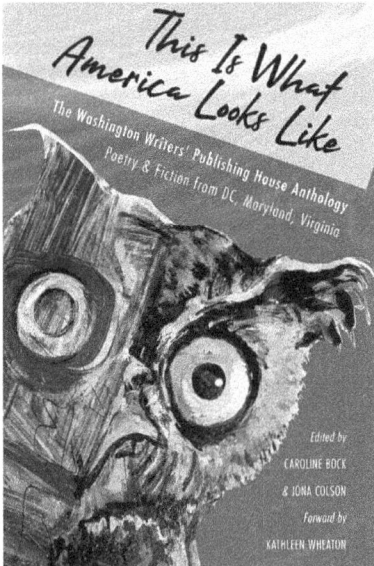

2020
Jean Feldman
Poetry Award

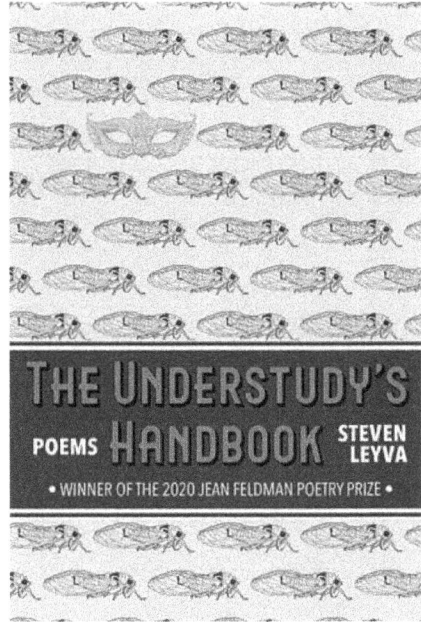

111 works of
short fiction and poetry
by 100 writers on the
creative state of America

More WWPH books here:

WWPH is an independent, nonprofit, cooperative press founded in 1975. Our mission is to publish and celebrate writers from DC, Maryland, and Virginia. To learn more about our fiction, poetry, and creative nonfiction manuscript contests, our bi-weekly literary journal, and to purchase more WWPH books, please visit:

www.washingtonwriters.org

Follow us on:
Twitter@wwphpress
Facebook@WWPH
Instagram@writingfromWWPH
Contact us at:
wwphpress@gmail.com

PROUD MEMBER

[clmp]

COMMUNITY OF LITERARY MAGAZINES & PRESSES
W W W . C L M P . O R G

WWPH is a proud recipient of a
Creativity Grant from

MSAC
DEPARTMENT OF COMMERCE maryland state arts council

www.ingramcontent.com/pod-product-compliance
Lightning Source LLC
Chambersburg PA
CBHW022029090426
42739CB00006BA/352